PROVE IT:
GATHERING EVIDENCE AND INTEGRATING INFORMATION

Miriam Coleman

PowerKiDS
press.

New York

Published in 2013 by The Rosen Publishing Group, Inc.
29 East 21st Street, New York, NY 10010

First Edition

Editor: Joanne Randolph
Book Design: Kate Laczynski
Layout Design: Holly Rankin

Photo Credits: Cover Datacraft Co Ltd/Getty Images; p. 4 Rob Marmion/Shutterstock.com; p. 5 Georgios Kollidas/Shutterstock.com; p. 6 James Steidl/Shutterstock.com; p. 7 © iStockphoto/Thinkstock; p. 8 © iStockphoto.com/comptine; p. 9 Tessa Codrington/Stone/Getty Images; p.10 Villiers Steyn/Shutterstock.com; p. 11 © iStockphoto.com/gbh007; p. 13 Hemera/Thinkstock; p. 15 Nicholas Kamm/Getty Images; p. 16 mlorenz/Shutterstock.com; p. 16 (bottom) © iStockphoto.com/bowdenimages; p. 18 JupiterImages /Pixland/Thinkstock; p. 19 Ken Lucas/Visuals Unlimited/Getty Images; p. 21 David Young-Wolff/ Riser/Getty Images; p. 22 Tim Kitchen/Riser/Getty Images; p. 24 David Oliver/ Taxi/Getty Images; p. 26 © iStockphoto.com/asiseeit p. 28 Richard Hutchings/Photo Researchers/Getty Images; p. 28 (inset) © iStockphoto.com/Violka08; p. 29 Ryan McVay/Lifesize/Thinkstock; p.30 Nick White/ Photodisc/Thinkstock.

Library of Congress Cataloging-in-Publication Data

Coleman, Miriam.
 Prove it : gathering evidence and integrating information / by Miriam Coleman. — 1st ed.
     p. cm. — (Core skills)
 Includes index.
 ISBN 978-1-4488-7453-8 (library binding) — ISBN 978-1-4488-7525-2 (pbk.) —
 ISBN 978-1-4488-7600-6 (6-pack)
 1. Report writing—Juvenile literature. 2. Research—Juvenile literature. I. Title.
 LB1047.3.C655 2013
 808.02—dc23
                                        2012006010

Manufactured in the United States of America

CPSIA Compliance Information: Batch #SW12PK: For Further Information contact Rosen Publishing, New York, New York at 1-800-237-9932

Contents

WHAT IS PROOF?

When you make claims in a report or research project, why should your readers believe you? Proof is the evidence you present in order to show that a statement is true.

Some facts are easy to prove. You can prove that one plus one equals two just by counting, but many

Science experiments are done to prove an idea, or theory. If your results can be repeated, then you have evidence your theory was correct.

The scientist Sir Isaac Newton used what he could see, such as the force acting on an apple that falls to the ground, to prove bigger ideas about gravity and the orbit of bodies in space.

facts and claims are more **complicated** and harder to prove. If you wanted to prove that Washington State grows the most apples in the United States, you would need to find data that measures and compares the number of apples produced by each state.

If you wanted to show that James Monroe was not an effective US president, finding proof would be even more complicated. You would need to review Monroe's career through historical records and later biographies. You would need to look at the policies he **enacted** and measure their success.

Some math problems are easy to prove because the objects they stand for are countable. Other math problems are harder to prove. Mathematicians must show their work and give evidence to support the answers they reach.

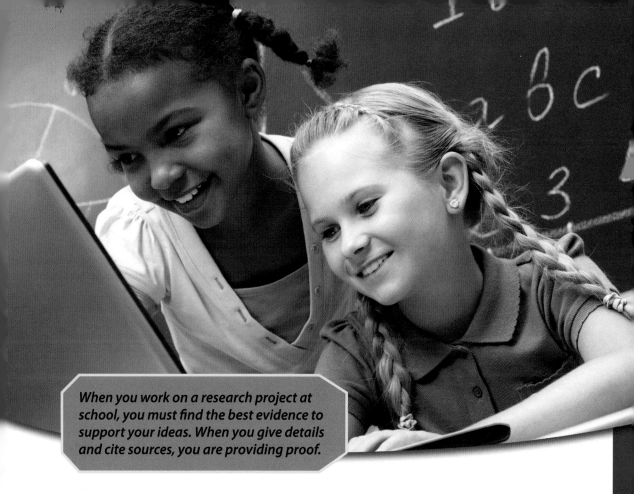

When you work on a research project at school, you must find the best evidence to support your ideas. When you give details and cite sources, you are providing proof.

You might even need to show that other leaders of Monroe's time did better jobs handling similar issues. Proof can come from a wide variety of sources. You can find proof in books and websites, in observations and experiments, and in **statistics** and surveys. Proof can even come from your own life experience.

WHY DO I NEED EVIDENCE?

Evidence plays an important role in our lives. We feel safe taking medicine because scientists have provided evidence proving that certain chemicals fight illness. We make most of our important decisions based on evidence that we have received from a variety of sources.

If your teacher asks you to find out why the sky is blue, you might make a guess. However, you need to do research using reputable sources, such as NASA's website, to find out the facts and support your ideas.

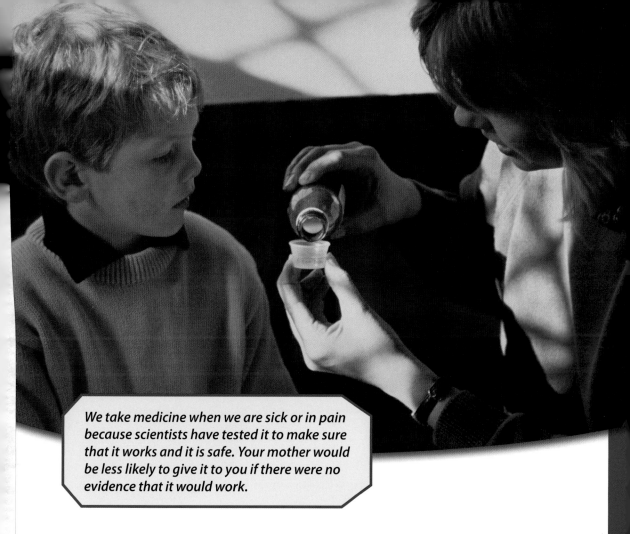

We take medicine when we are sick or in pain because scientists have tested it to make sure that it works and it is safe. Your mother would be less likely to give it to you if there were no evidence that it would work.

When you read a book or do a project for school, it is important to develop your own ideas and draw your own conclusions about the material. You should base these ideas and conclusions on information gathered from many different places. When you share these ideas and conclusions, you must present evidence to back up your claims.

Evidence gives strength to the points you make. It shows that you have learned enough about your subject to draw reasonable conclusions. It can also show that experts on the topic agree with you. It can convince your readers to accept your conclusions as the truth.

Scientists observe, or watch something closely, to gather evidence about some things, such as how a mother elephant cares for her baby. Other kinds of evidence are facts that can be measured. These might include how big an elephant grows or how much food it eats each day.

GATHERING DATA FROM BOOKS

Finding information in books **efficiently** is an important skill to learn. It allows you to build up a store of the evidence you need quickly. It also allows you to rule out books that do not have the information you seek quickly.

> Use the library catalog to find titles that will help you with your research. When you pull a book from the shelf, do a quick check of the contents to be sure the book covers the topics you need.

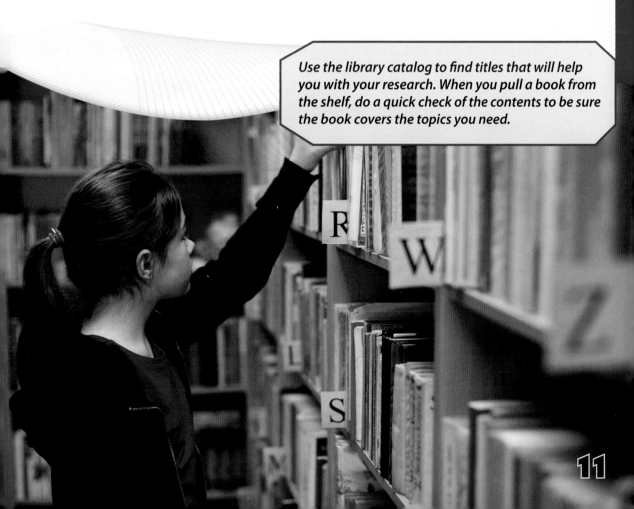

Looking at a book's table of contents is a good place to start since it tells you how the book is arranged and what subjects are covered in each chapter. A book's **index** can help you pinpoint exactly which pages have the facts you are looking for.

Books can also offer clues for finding more information from other sources. Many books contain bibliographies, which are lists of sources that that book's author used.

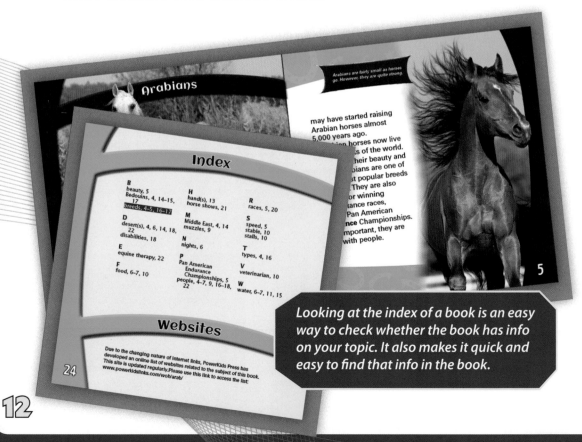

Looking at the index of a book is an easy way to check whether the book has info on your topic. It also makes it quick and easy to find that info in the book.

Bibliography

"The Wombat (Vombatus ursinus)." Australianfauna.com. February 2004. Retrieved December 28, 2009 <http://www.australianfauna.com/wombat.php>.

"Southern Hairy-Nosed Wombat." Chicago Zoological Society. 2009. Brookfield Zoo. Retrieved December 28, 2009 <http://www.brookfieldzoo.org/CZS/wombats>.

"Wombat." *Encyclopedia Britannica Online* 2009. Encyclopedia Britannica. Retrieved December 24, 2009 <http://search.eb.com/eb/article-9077371>.

Green, Emily. "*Lasiorhinus latifrons:* Southern Hairy-Nosed Wombat." *Animal Diversity Web.* 2009. Retrieved December 28, 2009 <http://animaldiversity.ummz.umich.edu/site/accounts/information/Lasiorhinus_latifrons.html>.

THE WATER CYCLE

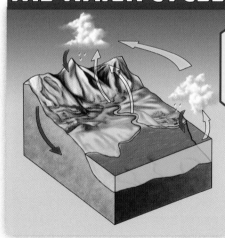

Diagrams and charts can give information, too. You can create a diagram on the water cycle based on the facts you learn from your research to show readers how the cycle works.

You can use a book's bibliography to find the most respected authorities on your subject. As you read through a book, take notes on keywords related to your topic. You can use these words to start a web search to find more sources.

GATHERING DATA FROM DIGITAL SOURCES AND OTHER MEDIA

You can gather data from digital sources in much the same way you find it in books. Typing keywords related to your topic into a search engine such as Google can quickly turn up millions of results. Digital databases are collections of

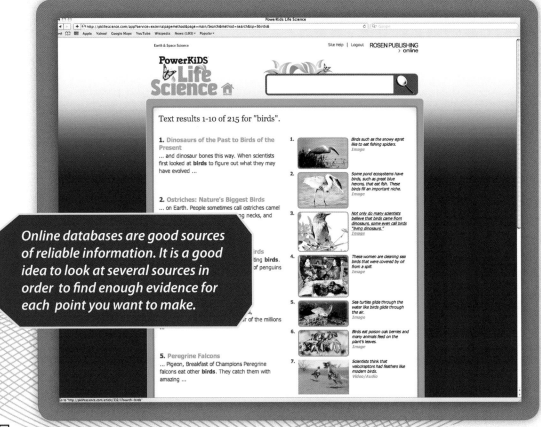

Online databases are good sources of reliable information. It is a good idea to look at several sources in order to find enough evidence for each point you want to make.

Google™

Advanced Sea
Language Too

[Google Search] [I'm Feeling Lucky]

Make G

Advertising Programs -

Your information is only as good as the facts you have. When you use a search engine, lots of sites come up. You need to look critically at the websites and decide which ones are reliable and will have facts to prove your ideas.

information that make it easy to find books, articles, and statistics related to your topic.

Videos and interviews that you conduct yourself can also provide a great deal of useful information. Always remember to take careful notes, no matter what type of source you are using.

QUICK TIP

Many of the sources that a search engine turns up will not be helpful or reliable. Look for websites of universities, museums, government agencies, and newspapers or magazines for reliable information.

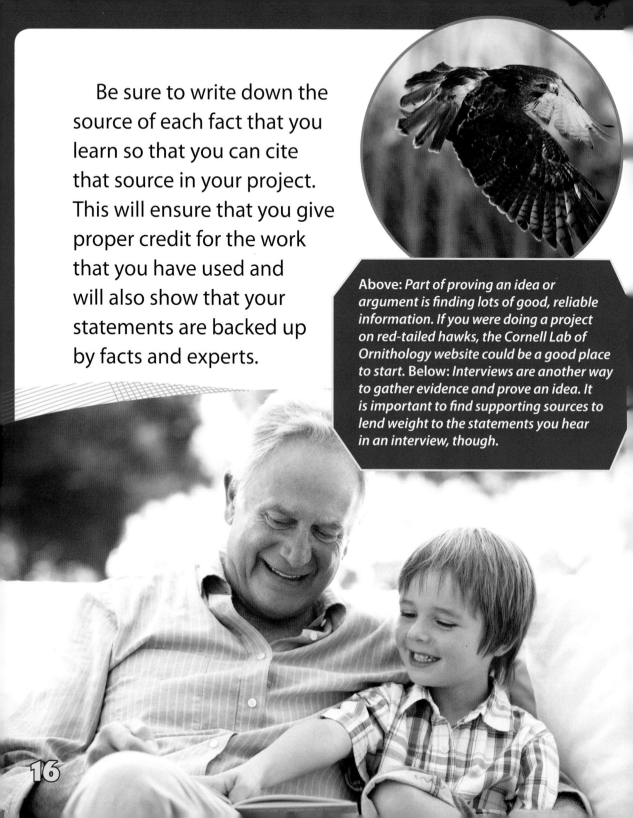

Be sure to write down the source of each fact that you learn so that you can cite that source in your project. This will ensure that you give proper credit for the work that you have used and will also show that your statements are backed up by facts and experts.

Above: *Part of proving an idea or argument is finding lots of good, reliable information. If you were doing a project on red-tailed hawks, the Cornell Lab of Ornithology website could be a good place to start.* **Below:** *Interviews are another way to gather evidence and prove an idea. It is important to find supporting sources to lend weight to the statements you hear in an interview, though.*

WHAT DOES IT ALL MEAN?

Once you find sources of information, it is important to look at them critically. A good source will present facts clearly and will be written by a person who is knowledgeable about the subject. It will cite sources so you can see where the information comes from. If it concerns a current topic, it will have been published recently.

QUICK TIP

Community-edited websites like Wikipedia are not generally a reliable source of information because anyone can write or change the text at any time. However, the footnotes and lists of sources at the bottom of each Wikipedia entry will often lead you to more reliable sources.

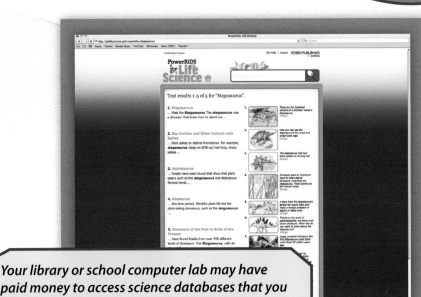

Your library or school computer lab may have paid money to access science databases that you can use for research. A science database generally has factual information on different topics.

Look carefully at your source to see if it could be biased. Is the publication or website **affiliated** with a political party or other organization that may want to present information in a way that benefits itself? Is the author or publication trying to sell you a product? Does the site focus on only one issue and give only one side of that issue? Does the language used seem unusually emotional? All of these are clues that the information presented might be biased.

Not everything we hear or read is true. Even when our best friends tell us things, it makes sense to find out more before we believe what they say is true.

If you research the stegosaurus, one source might say it was 26 feet (8 m) long. Another says it was 30 feet (9 m) long. Check a few more sources and then pick the number that makes the most sense based on the data you have.

Primary sources such as personal letters or news articles written at the time of a historical event often reflect the **prejudices** of their times. These sources can still be useful despite their biases since they offer valuable insight into history.

QUICK TIP

Another issue to look out for is **accountability**, especially when it comes to websites. Is anyone editing the website besides the person writing the article? Personal blogs, even those of experts, may be full of errors because there is no one else reading the blogs who can catch them.

MAKE YOUR ARGUMENT AND BACK IT UP

Once you have found all the information you need, it is time to draw your own conclusions and back them up. If you are writing an essay, start by introducing your topic and stating your main idea. This is called the thesis

QUICK TIP

Outlines are a good way to plan your project. Include your main ideas and the facts you will use to support them.

This is a piece of an outline you might make if your teacher asked you whether or not you think any of the predictions for the future in 2030: A Day in the Life of Tomorrow's Kids by Amy Zuckerman and Jim Daly would really be possible by 2030.

2030: A Day in the Life of Tomorrow's Kids Outline
I. What are the main ideas in this book?
    A. Technology
    B. Being ecofriendly
    C. Population growth and what it means
II. Is the technology in this book likely to be available in 2030?
    A. Explain my thoughts on whether some of the authors' ideas are possible
    B. Highlight some of the authors' proof
    C. Give my proof
III. Will life on Earth really be more ecofriendly?
    A. My thoughts
    B. Authors' proof
    C. My proof

English class is not the only class in which you will be asked to gather evidence, integrate information, and prove your ideas. Think about science class. You come up with a good guess for how something works or what might happen, and then you find evidence to prove it.

statement. You would start an oral presentation the same way.

In the body of the essay, back up your thesis statement with supporting paragraphs. A good essay will usually have at least three supporting paragraphs. Start each of these paragraphs with

QUICK TIP

Use linking phrases such as "for instance," "in order to," "in addition," and "because" to develop flow between your thesis and evidence.

a statement that supports your main thesis. Then support that statement with related evidence, using facts, statistics, or quotes to make your case. At the end of the essay, summarize your points and then write a conclusion. Oral presentations need to have supporting evidence, too.

Build in some time to think about the information you found in the different sources you used. How can you use this data to back up your ideas?

YOU CAN QUOTE ME!

In order to provide evidence for your claim, you will be providing many facts and details taken from other sources. Most of the time, you will be **paraphrasing** these sources and giving them credit either in footnotes, endnotes, or in-text citations.

There are times, however, when directly quoting your sources is the most effective way of presenting evidence. An expert may have already found the most persuasive language to use in describing the point you wish to make. Calling attention to the voice of an authority can also go a long way in convincing a reader. In

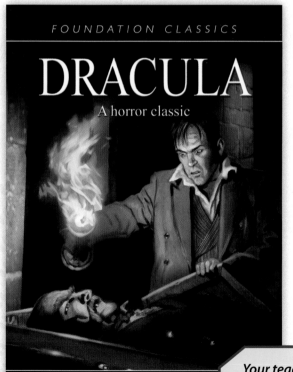

FOUNDATION CLASSICS

DRACULA
A horror classic

Original by Bram Stoker
Retold by Pauline Francis

Your teacher might ask you to write something about a fiction story you are reading. Quotes are a great way to support your ideas about what an author's main themes are in a book.

Take notes on your favorite lines in a text as you read or research online. Be sure to include why you feel the quotations you have picked stand out for you or are a good support for what you are trying to prove.

other cases, you might want to quote from a primary source to illustrate how people felt and thought at a particular time in history. In these cases, you will want to write in the text where the quote came from, in addition to providing the citation information in a note.

PUTTING IT ALL TOGETHER

Gathering data from many different sources and figuring out how it all fits together is the key to writing either a great persuasive essay or a great research project. By digging deeply into

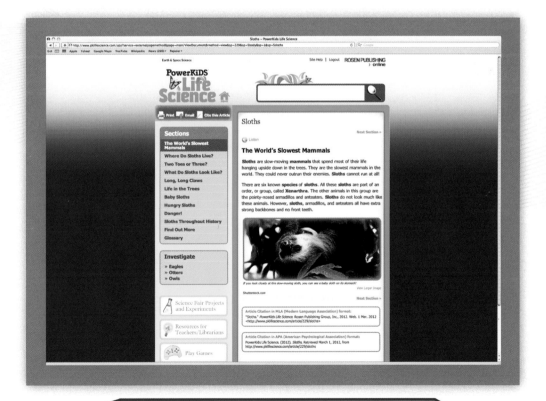

Use online and print sources for your projects to give you a well-rounded picture of the topic you are researching.

every type of source, from books and newspapers to websites and interviews, you should be able to learn enough about a subject to distinguish good sources from bad ones and to form your own conclusions.

> *You will feel confident turning in a project when you know you have done good research and proved your ideas.*

> While there are hundreds of sources online on different topics, it is important to use some print sources, too. Published books, like this one, are generally fact-checked and edited, so you can count on their information.

me to Eat!

Three-toed sloths are **herbivores**, or plant eaters. They eat mostly young leaves because they are easier to digest, or break down. They also will eat twigs, shoots, and fruit from the trees in which they live, though.

Sloths use their blunt cheek teeth to mash their food. Their stomachs have many chambers, or parts. This helps them digest, or break down, the plant material. A sloth has about half as much muscle as

Liana vines climb up rain forest trees and spread to other trees, too. Sloths eat the liana vine leaves, but they also use the vines to climb between trees in the canopy.

Sloths eat leaves and fruits from many trees, including cecropia, Mandevilla, Micropholis verulosa, and ficus trees.

other mammals of its size. Having less muscle mass means sloths do not need as much food energy. Luckily, sloths do not need a lot of muscle for their slow-moving lifestyle, so the sloth's diet is suited to its needs.

15

Organizing your information is an important step in developing an evidence-based argument that will be clear and persuasive to your reader. As you gather data from your sources, take careful notes

You can get a lot of information from graphic organizers. You can also put together a graphic organizer to show what you have learned about a topic. Graphic organizers are great tools for synthesizing information.

and think about how the facts relate to each other. Does a set of statistics from a government website help you understand what a historical diary tells you? Do the facts presented in a biography **contradict** what you learned in a magazine story? You might find it helpful to use a **graphic organizer** to help **integrate** everything you have learned.

Sometimes you will be asked to present what you have learned orally, or by speaking in front of the class. Just as you would in a written report, you will want to state your ideas clearly and give the evidence you found to back them up.

SKILLS FOR LIFE

Learning how to turn data into clear and organized evidence is not just a skill you use in school. It is something you will use your whole life. You will know how to choose the best sources of information in order to understand what is really going on in the world.

These skills will be important as you decide which college to apply to or what kind of mortgage you want when you are ready to buy a house one day. In your career, you will need to present your ideas and then prove them to your coworkers. You are learning skills that will support you throughout your life.

Remember that finding good sources and backing up your ideas with proof is teaching you a lot more than just history, science, or another topic. You are learning skills for life!

Glossary

accountability (uh-kown-tuh-BIH-luh-tee) Responsibility for someone's actions or words.

affiliated (uh-FIH-lee-ayt-ed) Associated with a group.

complicated (KOM-pluh-kayt-ed) Hard to understand.

contradict (kon-truh-DIKT) To say the opposite of something, disagree, or have a different opinion from another.

efficiently (ih-FIH-shent-lee) Done in the quickest, best way possible.

enacted (ih-NAKT-ed) Made into law.

graphic organizer (GRA-fik OR-guh-ny-zer) A chart, graph, or picture that sorts facts and ideas and makes them clear.

index (IN-deks) A list, usually found at the back of the book, that states what is in the book and on what page it can be found.

integrate (IN-tuh-grayt) To bring different parts together to form a whole.

paraphrasing (PER-uh-frayz-ing) Expressing the same meaning using different words.

prejudices (PREH-juh-dis-ez) Disliking a group of people different from you.

statistics (stuh-TIS-tiks) Facts in the form of numbers.

Index

Websites

Due to the changing nature of Internet links, PowerKids Press has developed an online list of websites related to the subject of this book. This site is updated regularly. Please use this link to access the list:
www.powerkidslinks.com/cs/prove/